PATTI
AT THE MUSIC SHOP

by Vítek Mecner

ALBATROS

To all children who love music.

Some children like to visit toy shops,
others prefer candy shops,
and there are some who like going to parks.
But a little girl named Patti loves to visit music shops.
One very special day, her dad took her
to the greatest music shop in town . . .

TOYS

"Hello!" Patti said to the shop clerk and asked,
"Excuse me, sir, where can I find the bass guitars, please?"
"Oh, those are up a floor," he said and pointed to the stairs.

On the way to the stairs,
Patti and her dad saw

many interesting instruments—guitars,
banjos, and mandolins.

Imagine all the beautiful instruments;
even Patti's dad could not resist playing one guitar.

Patti loved it so much, she also wanted to try!

So Patti tried playing:

The electric guitar

The piano

The triangle

The maracas

The pan flute

The trumpet

The tambourine

The harp

The balalaika

The harmonica

The theremin

She also tried on
different kinds of headphones.

The tuba

The xylophone

The cymbals

And the drums.

Patti wanted to play all the instruments!
Her favorite was the bass guitar.

MUSIC

They found the stairs going up to the second floor,
where all the bass guitars were.
The wall was decorated with posters of famous musicians,
vinyl records, and pictures of happy customers.

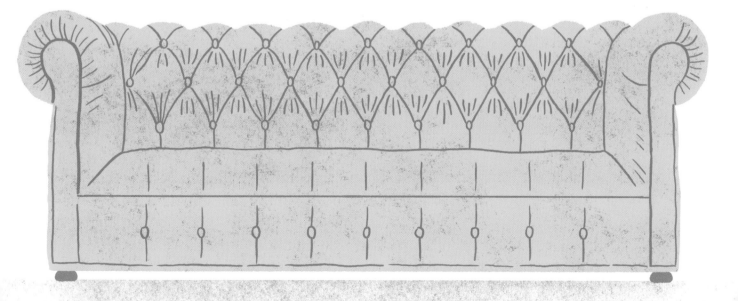

There it was—a beautiful red bass guitar!

But the bass guitar was too big for Patti to play.
Her fingers were too tiny to reach the strings.

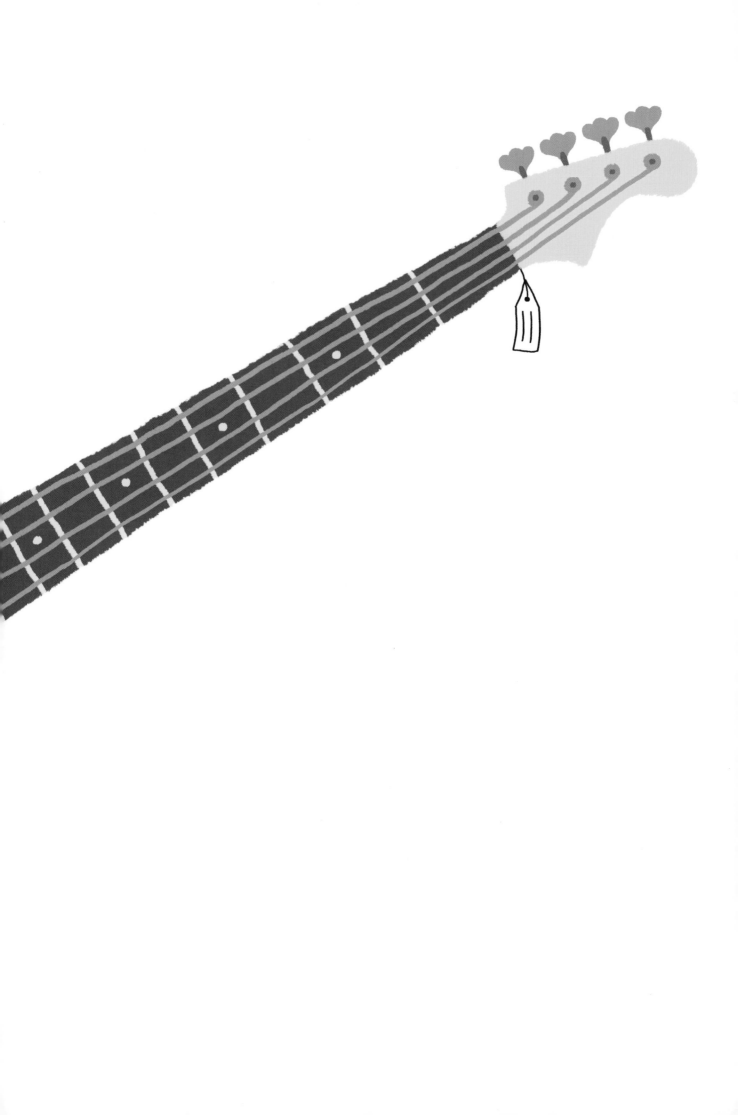

She was sad, because she really wanted to play the bass guitar!

But her dad had an idea.

"Patti, this is a ukulele," her dad said.
He gave her the little instrument.
"A ukulele has four strings, just like the bass guitar,
but it sounds a bit different, and it will fit your hands.
Would you like to try it?"

Patti saw that it looked like a small bass guitar!
She fell in love with the ukulele at first sight.

Patti loved the ukulele so much that her dad bought it for her.
Now she can practice until she grows big and can play the bass guitar.

THE END

PATTI AT THE MUSIC SHOP

© Albatros Media Group, 2022
5. května 1746/22, Prague 4, Czech Republic.

Text and Illustrations © Vítek Mecner, 2021
Translation: Irena Takahashi
Coordination and typesetting: Veronika Kopečková (MIMOTO)
Printed in China by Leo Paper Group.

978-80-00-06597-7

albatros